METHODISM AND THE TRADE UNIONS

*The Wesley Historical Lecture, No. 25
Methodist Conference, 1959
A Synopsis of which was delivered at
The New Room, Broadmead, Bristol
on 8th July 1959*

Methodism and the Common People of the Eighteenth Century

Methodism and the Working-class Movements, 1800-50

Some Working-class Movements of the Nineteenth Century

Methodism and the Struggle of the Working Classes, 1850-1900

The Social and Political Influence of Methodism in the Twentieth Century

Pages from a Padre's Diary

METHODISM AND THE TRADE UNIONS

by

ROBERT F. WEARMOUTH
M.A., B.Sc., Ph.D., F.M.H., H.C.F.

LONDON : THE EPWORTH PRESS

FIRST PUBLISHED IN 1959

© THE EPWORTH PRESS 1959

Book Steward
FRANK H. CUMBERS

SET IN MONOTYPE BASKERVILLE AND PRINTED IN
GREAT BRITAIN BY THE CAMELOT PRESS LTD
LONDON AND SOUTHAMPTON

PREFACE

What the working classes of this land owe to religion and to Methodism in particular has never been fully portrayed. Some attempt to assess its range and importance has been made in previous works, but much more needs to be done to complete the story, the half of which has never been told. Only one phase of Methodist influence on working-class activity is considered in this volume. Mainly because of restricted space the treatment of the subject is necessarily limited, and becomes little more than an introduction to, or a brief sketch of, important historical facts.

Sincere thanks are expressed to the Wesley Historical Society for asking me to write on this subject and for the promise to sponsor the publication. Where opinion is given it is my own and not of necessity that of the Society.

Hearty thanks also given to Sydney Walton, C.B.E., M.A., B.Litt., for reading the typescript, making suggestions, and checking the proof, and to my neighbour T. G. Dalziel for help in reading the proofs.

ROBERT F. WEARMOUTH

CONTENTS

CHAPTER ONE

THE BACKGROUND OF THE TRADE UNIONS: CONDITION OF WORKING CLASSES

IN ORDER TO understand the relation between Methodism and the Trade Unions one must know something about the background of Trade Unionism together with its purpose and progress.

The condition of the working classes in the nineteenth century fills up most of the background. They had to face

I. ECONOMIC DEPRESSION AND RECESSION

An economic depression may be regarded as a defect of national economy, an evil to be eradicated, a phenomenon to be exorcised. Call it a traffic jam—a local one, a national one, yea an international one—with many bottlenecks.

Pharaoh's society in the days of Joseph the dreamer was infected with this complaint. According to King Pharaoh's dreams 'the ill-favoured and lean-fleshed kine did eat up the seven well-favoured and fat kine'. 'The seven thin ears devoured the seven rank and full ears.' Joseph recognized the economic significance of these phenomena and predicted a depression that would consume the seven years' fruits of prosperity. He accordingly advised his master to provide for the coming emergency so strangely portrayed.[1]

There have been depressions all along the ages. In a free enterprise it is very difficult to avoid recessions and depressions. They seem to be part of the hazards of freedom.

Whatever may be the cause there can be no doubt about the results. The whole nation suffers when there is less

[1] Genesis 41.

buying, less selling, and less production. The business-man suffers loss of income and in some cases faces bankruptcy. The working classes suffer the most; in many cases they suffer loss of health and strength and even life itself.

Depressions in the past have come at regular intervals; for instance, in 1800-1, 1816, 1826, 1829, 1837-8, 1842, 1847, 1856-8.

Between 1851 and 1861 farmers in England suffered at least five bad seasons, 1853, 1855, 1859, 1860, 1861, the average production per acre falling to twenty-four bushels.[2] This was followed by a slump in the cotton industry, occasioned mainly by the civil war in America. Numerous mills went out of production and thousands of operatives became workless and destitute. Preston and Blackburn suffered severely. The Wesleyan Church joined in the general relief work and assisted twenty-five thousand souls.

A worse depression came in the 'seventies and the 'eighties, returning again in the 'nineties. 'Six bad seasons in succession', 'No good harvest since 1874', 'A deficient yield of corn', 'An absence of sunshine', 'Low prices', 'Losses in live-stock', 'Foreign competition'; these were the laments of the farmers. All counties south of Durham and Lancashire suffered severely.

Industry suffered a recession in 1884, 1885, 1886. Another depression came to agriculture in 1891-3 and was regarded as 'worse—far worse than that of thirteen or fourteen years ago'.[3]

The most disastrous depression in English Social History came in 1929-33, preceded by a long recession from 1922 to 1929. Whole villages in the counties of Northumberland and Durham and South Wales seemed to be out of work.

The working classes had to endure

---

[2] *Report of Royal Commission on Agriculture* (P.P. 1882), XIV.11.
[3] Ibid. (1894), XVI.5.

II. SHORT TIME AND UNEMPLOYMENT

In the time of depression the employer usually reduces the
number of his workmen or he might employ the same
number on a shortened week. In a traffic jam, movement
has nearly stopped for a time, or it might be forced into
a crawl. The exchange of goods is consequently slowed
down. That kind of thing happens on a larger scale when
the depression arrives. Everything seems to be slowed
down. There is less work for the workmen and fewer men
are employed.

No statistics have been provided to show the state of
unemployment in the early years of the nineteenth
century. Miscellaneous reports, however, show the real
state of the workless. In regard to Lancashire, an index
of other counties, a report from Manchester in 1847
asserts that 'the total number of mills in the vicinity
engaged in full time was 84 out of 175'.[4] 'In Preston,
Bolton, and Ashton, only 28 mills out of 153 employed
all their workmen.' Another report averred that '50 per
cent of the mill hands' in Lancashire were out of work.
Similar conditions prevailed in Staffordshire.

Many of the Trade Unions provided for their unemployed and kept accounts of their numbers. The Iron
Founders had the following numbers out of work, in
1855, 10 per cent; 1858, 16; 1862, 13·8; 1867, 15·9; 1868,
18; 1869, 15·5; 1878, 14·6; 1879, 22·3; 1880, 10·9;
1885, 10·9; 1886, 13·9; 1887, 10.'[5]

The Amalgamated Engineers in 1853 had 0·8 per cent
unemployed; in 1879 they had 13·3 per cent.[6]

One observer in 1896 declared that 'Bristol was crowded
with the unemployed'. Liverpool had 'thousands of men

[4] Wearmouth, *Methodism and the Struggle of the Working Classes*, p. 137.
[5] *Fifth Report on Trade Unions* (1891, P.P. 1893-4), CII.80.
[6] *Second Report of Trade Unions* (1888), CVII.30.

walking the streets in a starving condition, owing to their inability to obtain employment'. Shaftesbury 'was in a most dreadful condition owing to slackness of work and low wages'. Keir Hardie estimated the number of unemployed in the United Kingdom at two million, and with those dependent on them at six million.[7]

The number of those on short time approximated to that of the unemployed. As there was no sign of an easement of the problem the Liberal Government brought into the House of Commons a system of State Insurance against unemployment and sickness, preceded by the first instalment of Old Age Pensions introduced in 1908. The highest point in unemployment was reached in 1929-31 when the number for the first time passed the three million mark.

To visualize the state of the unemployed one must remember there was no compulsory insurance of any kind before 1908. There was nothing but private charity and the meagre allowance from the Poor Law fund.

The working classes had to accept

III. LONG HOURS AND LOW WAGES

It was generally agreed that an employer could do what he liked with his business, his factory, his money, and his workmen. With the employers the idea clung tenaciously and long. The matter apparently was not disputed until the Trade Unions demanded a share in the fixing of wages, hours of work, and conditions of employment. As a rule the employer fixed a very low standard of wage, the lowest possible, and the maximum number of hours per day.

In agriculture wages were never high. According to the *Report on the Earnings of the Agricultural Labourer*: 'Over the period 1850-99 wages had gone up in Suffolk from

[7] *Report of Select Committee on Distress* (1896), Vol. IX.

10s. to 12s.; in Essex 9s. to 12s.; Hampshire 9s. to 12s.; Wiltshire 7s. to 12s.; Somerset 7s. to 12s.; Gloucestershire 7s. 6d. to 12s.'[8]

Wages among industrial workers also varied from time to time and from place to place. In the early 'nineties a Report stated that 'Rather less than 24 per cent earn under 20s., and about 17 per cent above 30s.'[9] At the end of the century a large number of wage-earners were still receiving less than 20s. a week.

Hours among agricultural labourers were notoriously long. From 1850 to 1890 they varied from county to county. In Norfolk they averaged 57 a week; in Northumberland 63 in the summer and 60 in winter; in Durham 60 and 54; in Yorkshire 63 and 54; in Lincolnshire 66 and 54. According to another Report the twelve-hour day had been established in fifteen counties.

The ten-hour day had been legalized in 1847 and the agitation for still shorter hours was carried forward. The miners in Durham and Northumberland gained a seven-hour day in 1890, but other workers were not so fortunate. Dockers in 1890 laboured 53 to 57 hours. Railway men had to work 54 to 73. The general tendency, however, was toward a shorter day and the movement for an eight-hour day gathered momentum. In 1899 26,082 people secured the eight-hour day and in the following year 57,726.

When I was a student at the London School of Economics I was requested on one occasion to write an essay on the 'Minimum Number of Hours to work to Obtain the Maximum Production'. In my investigations I examined the statistics of various industries and ascertained these facts. The best production in the heavy industries could be obtained at seven hours a day; in the

[8] (1900), LXXXII.37, 238-50.
[9] *Royal Commission on Labour* (1894), XXXV.10.

clerical departments eight hours; in other forms of labour
between seven and eight hours a day.

The highest production during the twenty-four hours is
from 9 a.m. to 12, the lowest from 12 p.m. to 3 a.m. The
working classes in the nineteenth and twentieth centuries
were far from that standard. They had to work longer
hours, which was contrary to human nature and economic
laws.

IV. HIGH PRICES AND A POOR DIET

The working classes had to pay high prices for their food
stuffs and exist on a low diet. With meagre wages when
fully employed, and no wages when out of work, and a
poor wage when partly employed, the labouring portions
of the community could not afford the luxury of high
prices, and in consequence they had to subsist on a low
diet. Bread and potatoes were important items in a
worker's diet and they were rather costly at any time,
and more so before the repeal of the corn laws in 1844.
During the Napoleonic wars the price of wheat went up
to 150·3s. a quarter.

Herein is a list of food prices in vogue in 1815: Tea 6s.
a lb; sugar 9½d., coffee 1s. 11d.; currants 10½d.; butter
1s. 2d.; cheese 9d.; bacon 8½d. Boots and shoes were 14s.
a pair.

Reports to the Home Office often carried complaints
about the rise in prices. At a meeting in Oldham in 1811
of clergymen, manufacturers, and inhabitants on 12th
November, it was decided to send a petition to the Prince
Regent acquainting him of the advance 'in the price of
flour, meal, and potatoes'.[10] General Maitland, Com-
mander of the troops in the Midlands at that time con-
cluded that the real cause of the riots in 1811 was 'the
high price of provisions'.[11]

Similar complaints were made in 1839 by the Man-

[10] H.O. 42, 117 (1811).   [11] H.O. 40, 123 (1812).

chester Working Men's Association. 'We are compelled', they bitterly exclaimed, 'by the Government to purchase coffee at two shillings per pound instead of sixpence, to buy sugar at seven-pence or eight-pence per pound instead of three-pence, tea at four or five shillings when we could purchase it at one shilling and three-pence. . . . Bread, too, we are compelled to buy somewhat about double its value.'[12]

To one of the Government Commissioners a woman confessed that they never had tea at their house, only hot water and crusts. Women in Norfolk had to accustom themselves to that kind of diet. They could afford nothing better.

Joseph Skevington, the son of a Primitive Methodist Minister (The father shared in the making of the laws for the Primitive Methodist Connexion. He was one of the delegates at the Preparatory Meeting in Nottingham in 1819), reported from Loughborough in 1840 that many of the people there had to feed on stolen turnips to keep them from starving.

Another Primitive Methodist tells the story that when he was a boy he had to go to the workhouse for a time with the rest of the family because his father had been sent to gaol for stealing turnips to provide supper for his wife and children.

The working classes had to suffer

V. OVERCROWDING AND INSANITATION

Overcrowding and insanitation were closely related to the increase of population. When the first census was taken in 1801 the number of souls in England and Wales counted 8,890,000. In 1851 the number had risen to 17,928,000, an increase of over 9,000,000. In 1901 the number had reached 32,528,000.

Most of the industrial areas of the North and the

12 H.O. 40, 43 (1839).

Midlands had big increases. So had Middlesex and London.

To provide accommodation for all these extra people houses had to be built somehow and somewhere. As there was no central planning or sanitation authority houses were just built anyhow anywhere. Most people wanted to be near their work. They could not afford either time or money for much travelling. So houses were erected near the coal mines, the factories, the shops, and the blast furnace. They were tossed up with little thought of sunshine, fresh air, or water supply. As a matter of fact they were built for profit, sometimes back to back, with cesspools in front of the houses and open drains behind. As a consequence hundreds of thousands of working folk had to live in the midst of dirt, filth, vermin, and insanitation.

Many of the labouring population could not even procure a house; they had to live in cellars. Liverpool had 39,000 people who lived in 7,800 cellars. The great proportion of these cellars were dark, damp, dismal, confined, ill-ventilated and dirty.[13] Liverpool had the reputation of being 'the most unhealthy town of England'.[14]

Manchester had 15,000 people living in cellars. 'Among these cellar dwellings there were 1500 cases in which three persons slept in one bed; 738 cases where four slept in one bed, 281 cases where five slept in one bed, 94 cases where six slept in one bed, 27 cases where seven slept in one bed, 2 cases where eight slept in one bed, and 31 cases where there was no bed.'[15]

In many areas drainage was decidedly bad. Water supply was generally deficient. Some of the courts and alleys had no privies and no covered drains. The case of Wild Court, Drury Lane, London, provides an insight into the conditions of the time, 1854. Wild Court had 13

[13] *Report on Large Towns* (1845).
[14] *First Report on State of Towns* (1844).   [15] Ibid. (1845), Second Report.

houses with 13 privies and 16 cesspools and 100 rooms for 1000 people. The Labourer's Friend Society with Lord Shaftesbury as the chairman decided to purchase those 13 houses, pull them down, and build better ones without charging any additional rent. But when the workmen saw all the filth in the cesspools and in the houses they went on strike. By and by, being induced to work, they carted out of those cesspools 150 loads of filth, and from inside the houses 330 loads of refuse, and in addition to all this *one ton of bugs*.

The sanitary reformers of those days used to aver that 'there lies under London as much filth as would make a lake six feet in depth, a mile long, and a thousand feet across.'[16]

The lodging-houses were no better. In one room in St Giles 16 souls 'were found huddled together in a most filthy state'. In another room in Radcliff '15 were found in a most deplorable condition, 11 sleeping on the floor covered by a few filthy rags'. Another room in St Giles, 14 feet by 14½, had 'no less than 37 men, women, and children' 'all lying together on the floor like beasts'.[17]

In Alfred Row, London, a house with 48 rooms, containing a separate family in almost every room, had to depend on one open barrel 21 inches in diameter and 12 inches deep, situate under the same roof as the privy, for their supply of water.

Another observer called attention to 'a dark, dismal alley—tenanted by the outcasts of society—fetid with the reeking odour of undrained houses and uncovered cesspools'. There was 'no means of ventilation', the air being 'breathed and re-breathed, polluted and re-polluted—the floor a filthy pool. . . . The beds themselves swarming with the vilest and guiltiest of the population; and into each of them four, five, six, seven, and in some cases, eight,

---

[16] *Labourer's Friend Society Magazine* (1855), p. 144.
[17] Ibid. (1857), p. 157.

are thrust—no distinction of sex attempted—hoary ruffians
and girls, fathers and mothers—brothers and sisters—
married and unmarried—the sick and the healthy—all
without one thought of self-respect that even a savage
might inculcate, wedged in together to inhale and
generate fever, and, to imbibe a yet deadlier moral
pollution'.[18]

Reports from the provinces revealed conditions almost
as bad: 140 families lived in 34 houses in Blenheim
Street, Newcastle upon Tyne; in Blandford Street, 230
families in 50 houses; in George Street, 310 families in 62
houses.[19]

The working classes had to bear

VI. SICKNESS AND DISEASE

When one visualizes the dirt, filth, vermin, over-crowding,
and the insanitation, one is not surprised to hear of sickness and disease. No statistics were compiled in those days
to show the amount of sickness from place to place, but
there can be no doubt about the fact. Liverpool for
example was described as 'one of the most prosperous'
and also 'one of the most unhealthy towns in the kingdom'. 'Manchester was next in prosperity as well as
unhealthiness.'

When the cholera came to England in 1831-2 it 'raged
principally among the lower orders, . . . most of them
surviving only a few hours'. When it came to Sunderland
538 persons were stricken and 205 died. In Gateshead
402 were attacked and 144 died. In Newcastle 901 were
smitten and 306 died. In North Shields, Tynemouth,
Chirton, and Newburn 300 died. Altogether in the four
areas 2,141 were infected with the plague and 955
succumbed.

As there were so many ill-ventilated and dirty places in

18 *Labourer's Friend Society Magazine* (1851), p. 203.
19 *Report on Housing* (1884-5), Vol. XXX.

Newcastle calculated to spread the infection, landlords were requested by the authorities of the town to wash their houses with hot lime. The magistrates also took action and ordered the lanes in Sandgate to be washed with hot lime and to be thoroughly cleansed.

The plague came back to England in 1853-4. Newcastle suffered severely. One in 60 of the town population died of the fever, 1500 in nine weeks. When the Commissioners published their Report on the cholera in Newcastle they had some strong things to say about the town. They put it on record that Newcastle contained some of the worst insanitary features of the old-walled towns.

The house accommodation for the poorer folk was exceedingly defective. They were not only ill-lodged but exceedingly over-crowded. The Corporation as property-owners were worse than the private landlords. Houses were ill-constructed and ill-ventilated. There was want of proper drainage, sewage, and domestic convenience. The system of sewers was very defective and inefficient. There was deficiency in privy accommodation. Many of the streets were unpaved, uncleansed, filthy, and repulsive. The water supply to Newcastle from the Whittle Dean Water Company appeared to be almost universally complained of as 'bad', 'very bad', 'extremely or shockingly bad', 'much discoloured', 'turbid', 'perfect muddle', 'highly objectionable', 'unfit for drinking'.

Among the lower classes there were some of the most reckless and filthy beings it is possible to conceive.[20] In regard to Gateshead the Report declared that 'a large part of the dwellings of the poorer classes' were 'unfit for human habitation'.

In the two invasions of the plague to England over 90,000 people died. With the advance of medical science the plagues from the East had few victims in the following years, but sickness continued a terrible menace. At last in

[20] *Report on the Cholera in Newcastle upon Tyne* (1854).

1911 the Government brought in a scheme of National Insurance against sickness, and some of its effects were softened accordingly.

The working classes had to live in

VII. POVERTY AND DISTRESS

Low wages and high prices caused much poverty and distress, but ignorance and improvidence played their part.

For evidence of the extent of poverty and distress one can examine the Poor Law returns. These were published in statistical form every year and they show that in the course of the nineteenth century nearly one million people every week were receiving help from the Poor Law fund.

Evidence can be taken from Reports to the Home Office from various localities. In 1816 a meeting in London considered 'the widespread poverty of the labouring classes'. About the same time the Mayor of Leeds admitted that the distress in that town was never before equalled. The Vicar of Brosseley informed the Home Secretary that 30,000 colliers and furnace men were enduring 'the utmost distress'. Dr Grey of Sunderland told the Home Office 'that hundreds of the starving population' intended to injure him. In 1819 a local preacher at a public meeting represented the sufferings of the poor to be like that of the Israelites in Egypt. Francis Place, a great friend of the working classes, said in 1837 that 'a great mass of . . . unskilled and semi-skilled and skilled labourers are in great poverty and privation all their lives'.

The chief creative factor in the re-birth of the Birmingham Political Union in 1837 was 'the sufferings of the industrial classes'. The first petition of the Chartists in 1839 called attention to the starving condition of the labouring classes. In the 'hungry forties' the distress of the poor became more and more alarming. A petition from the power-loom weavers in Manchester to the Home Secretary declared that their sufferings were beyond human endurance. The piece-work knitters in Leicester told the chief constable of the town that 'dire necessity' compelled them to beg in the streets. 'All we want', they declared, 'is bread for our wives and families who are pining for want'.

In 1848 the Mayor of Manchester wrote to the Home Office to say that 'all classes have suffered, but the pressure has fallen most heavily on the working classes'.[21]

When Charles Booth investigated the condition of the poor in London (1886-90) he described them as 'dreadfully poor', 'an awfully poor, low, wretched lot—children almost naked', 'scarcely a rag to cover themselves', 'very dirty, untidy', 'improvident', 'houses in a dilapidated condition'.[22] 'About eleven thousand of the lowest class lived the life of savages. . . . Their food is of the coarsest description.' 'Poplar had 20,199 of the very poor, Bethnal Green 19,005; Hackney 13,976. . . . The 100,000 of very poor are at all times more or less in want.'[23] 'Taking the whole of London there were 37,610 of the very lowest and 316,834 very poor.'[24]

Evidence of distress was found in other records. In 1895 a *Report of the Royal Commission on the Aged Poor*, deplored the fact that 'so large a portion of the working classes are in old age in receipt of poor law relief'. There was exceptional distress in many places.

The working classes had to risk

VIII. STARVATION AND EARLY DEATH

In theory no one in England had need to die of starvation

---

[21] *H.O. Papers* (1811-50).   [22] *Labour and Life of the People*, I.3-17.
[23] Ibid. p. 22.   [24] Ibid.

or be in want of food. He had the right to go to the parish of his birth and demand sustenance. In practice, however, things were different. Throughout the whole of the nineteenth century thousands of people were on the verge of starvation. From 1868 to 1918 fifty-one *Reports* were published by the Government showing the number of people who died of starvation or whose death was accelerated by starvation. Nearly 3,000 cases were recorded. Here are a few examples: John Cook, aged 44, picture-frame maker; Jury's verdict on the cause of death: 'Exhaustion from insufficient nourishment.' Sarah Mills, 43, wife of hawker: 'Starvation.' James William Alley, 64, newsvendor: 'Starvation.' Timothy Flynn, 30, seaman: 'Starvation and exposure.' So the story goes on. A large number actually died in the open street.[25]

The fact that no *Reports* were available for the years prior to 1868 cannot be taken as evidence that nobody died of starvation. Many unreported deaths from starvation must have taken place. News from other sources bear witness. The *Reports* on *The State of Population in Large Towns, The Health of Towns, The Sanitary Condition of Large Towns, Pauperism,* and *The Aged Deserving Poor* provided a shock to many people. Without any doubt whatever the life of the working man was full of hazard. According to one *Report* 'the average life of the working classes in Liverpool was fifteen years, in Manchester seventeen, in Bolton eighteen, in Leeds nineteen, while in the Metropolis it was twenty-two'.[26]

Apart from their social significance the mortality figures had a theological effect. This might explain why eschatology assumes such a large and important place in the teaching and preaching of the nineteenth century.

Other facts can be added. For example the conditions

[25] *Reports on Death from Starvation* (1868-1918).
[26] *Report on the State of Large Towns* (1845).

in coal-mines. A large proportion of the persons employed in coal-mines were under the age of thirteen. Children began to work at the age of four. Female children were engaged under the same conditions as males. Parish apprentices were often employed without pay. Ventilation and drainage were lamentably defective. Some of the work meant solitary confinement. Both sexes were usually employed together, even in places where men worked almost naked. The hours of labour were never less than eleven, and often fourteen and upwards. Accidents were numerous and of a fearful nature. The main cause was lack of superintendence. A large number of young people received fatal injuries.

Individual evidence showed that in the West Riding a man took his child to work at the age of three. 'When the child was exhausted it was carried home, stripped, and put to bed.' A similar case occurred in a mine at Halifax. A child of three was made to follow its father into the workings 'to hold the candle, and when exhausted with fatigue was cradled upon the coals until his return at night'.

In some of the Yorkshire mines men worked in 'a state of perfect nakedness', and were 'in this state assisted in their labour by females of all ages, from girls of six years to women of twenty-one, these females being themselves quite naked down to the waist.

Girls were often employed at pulling or 'hurrying', that is pulling the baskets or wagons of coal along the ground by means of a long chain. Like a four-legged animal, these half-naked girls, creeping on their hands and feet with the chain between their legs, were compelled to go hither and thither for many hours on their burdensome task. When the road was wet they often had to pass through dirty water and filthy clay. Two girls in one pit had worn large holes in their trousers.

One woman confessed that she worked in the mine while 'in the family way'. Two of her children were born in the mine. One of the unfortunates was brought up the pit shaft in her dirty skirt.[27]

Other factors must go on the picture. For instance these working-class folk had no political power. They had few political rights. They had no representative in the House of Commons and no voice in the administration of affairs. They had no right of association, no right of public meeting, no right of the franchise, no right of equal justice, no right of State assistance except through the hated Poor Law.

Political rights were not acquired by magical processes, by the waving of the wand; nor were they the gifts of the gods or the favours of the fairies. They had to come by striving and struggling, struggling against the State, against the employers, and against the rulers of the land. They were the helpless victims of aristocratic laws.

Under the Poor Laws the poverty-sticken people were called paupers and treated accordingly. If they had to enter the workhouse the father went one way, the mother another, and the children somewhere else. The family tie was broken and the members were punished for their poverty.

Under the Settlement Laws no parish was obliged to support a poor man if he belonged to another parish. If he needed assistance he had to go back to the place of his birth and get help there. Many were the people that died on that journey.

Under the Vagrant Laws a person found begging in the streets was liable to be cast into jail.

Under the Penal Laws thousands of people were transported across the seas never to return again. Many of them were sold as slaves. Others might be hung in

[27] *First Report of Children in Mines* (1842), pp. 12-24.

public for the crime of stealing 2*d*., or 4*d*., or 6*d*., or 1*s*. There were 250 offences for which a person could be put to death by hanging.

Under the Trade Union Laws working men were not allowed to work out their own salvation by acting together. Each man had to make his own contract of hours and wages.

Under the Master and Servant Laws many an honest labourer was sent to prison to hard labour because some magistrate had erred in the meaning of the laws and had failed to administer justly.

The working classes had nothing to do with the making of the laws and nothing to do with their administration. They had to obey, of course, or disobey at their peril.

All these factors taken separately reveal a condition of things that even the novelist, Charles Dickens, could not describe in his *Hard Times*, and *Oliver Twist*. When the factors are taken together they depict a state of life almost unbelievable. Nevertheless, the facts are there to be examined, dispassionately or otherwise. One can find them in contemporary newspapers, in letters to the Home Office, in Government *Reports*, and in literature of various kinds.

Further still, education was neither free nor compulsory, nor was it universal. Consequently large numbers of the toiling masses were untutored, being unable to read or write.

Amenities were few and far between. They had no free public baths, no libraries, no reading-rooms, no parks, no recreation grounds. This was the position in the early part of the nineteenth century and some improvement was made in amenities before the end of the century. Nevertheless the half has never been told, nor will it ever be told.

It must not be assumed that the working classes were

satisfied with their lot. They were far from satisfied, and they tried to remedy the situation by appeals to the employers, petitions to the House of Commons, the organizing of political agitation, and the institution of the system of self-help in the form of Trade Unions.

CHAPTER TWO

THE PURPOSE AND PROGRESS OF
THE TRADE UNIONS

THE first Trade Unions had a twofold purpose, social and economic. The ethical and political purpose came later as something added or tacked on, something necessary, natural, and ultimately inevitable.

Some of the early Trade Unions of the nineteenth century had a Friendly Society basis. By united effort members of the unions provided financial benefit in times of sickness, unemployment, accident, old age, and decease. That objective seemed innocent enough. Nobody could object to it. In fact it was most laudable and praiseworthy. Most of the money subscribed by members went for Friendly Society benefits. That was a fact not generally recognized, but the Government *Reports* have left no doubt about the matter.

When the Commissioners published their *Report on the Rules and Organization of Trade Unions* in 1869, they definitely acknowledged that the social objective came first in the Trade Union programme; namely, 'to afford relief to the members of the Union when incapacitated from work by accident or sickness; to allow a sum for the funeral expenses of the members and their wives; and sometimes to provide superannuation allowance for members incapacitated by old age'. They confessed that in many cases the Trade Union appeared to be another name for Friendly Society. Year by year the amount of money spent on Friendly Society benefits far outweighed the total expended on strikes. It was also recognized by the Commissioners that the Unions were doing the work which the State, employers, and rate-payers should have been doing. Trade Unions were in reality making large contributions to the maintenance of the poor and unfortunate among their members. To that extent the draw on the National Budget, the Poor Rates, and the resources of employers was less.[1]

The Commissioners further admitted that 'Trade Unions have conferred great benefits on the working classes and the public generally through their expenditure for benefit purposes'. A later report in 1895 made the same assertion that Trade Unions nearly always provide superannuation benefits for their members, the primary object being to keep members from having to apply for Poor Law Relief.

Regardless of the fact that Trade Unions had a Friendly Society basis and objective they were banned by the State and opposed by employers. Common Law and Statute Law made all Trade Unions illegal. The Combination Acts of 1799 and 1800 were in force until 1824-5 and the Webbs (Sidney and Beatrice) describe this period as 'one of unmitigated persecution and continuous repression'. 'Thousands of journeymen suffered for the crime of combination.' 'Justice was out of the question.' Crowds of honest working men had to languish in jail for many weeks simply because they decided to act in unison to improve wages and working conditions. In 1816 seven scissors-grinders were sent to jail for three months for combining to form a Trade Union. In the following year ten delegates of the calico-printers union were incarcerated for three months. Some Bolton weavers in 1818 got two years. A year later some cotton-spinners were tried for conspiracy and eventually sent to jail. In the same year numerous prosecutions took place among the cabinet-makers, hatters, ironfounders, and other journeymen.[2]

[1] *Report of Commissioners on the Rules and Organization of Trade Unions* (1869).
[2] S. & B. Webb, *History of Trade Unionism*, pp. 73-81.

Even after the repeal of the Combination Acts in 1824-5 when Trade Unions were allowed to consider hours of work, wages, and conditions, the unions had no security for their funds, property, or organization. Any unscrupulous person could defraud them or cause damage to their buildings, and there was no redress, nor any punishment for the wrongdoer.

The opposition to Trade Unions was so fierce and bitter during the first half of the nineteenth century that very few combinations could survive. They were too weak to live. A classical example was provided by the experience of the Tolpuddle Martyrs.

Even the big unions were forced to surrender. The miners of Northumberland and Durham suffered defeat in the strikes of 1832 and 1844. Yorkshire, Lancashire, and the Midlands had a similar experience, and the Miners Association of Great Britain and Ireland, formed at Wakefield in 1842, had to dissolve. So had the Grand Union of all the Operative Spinners of the United Kingdom, the National Association for the Protection of Labour, the Builders Trade Union, the National Associated Smiths Union, the Grand Consolidated Trades Union of Great Britain and Ireland, and the National Union of Working Classes.

It was in this period and under these circumstances that the ethical purpose took shape and form. Ethical terms and connotations began to be employed, and Trade Union activities took on a moral garb. What the various unions wanted was a higher standard of life for their members and financial benefits in times of misfortune. All this could be regarded as fair, right, and just. To resist was unfair, wrong, and unjust.

To see Trade Unions dressed in the garments of compassion, kindness, justice, righteousness, consideration for the unfortunate, and bearing one another's burdens, had a tremendous effect upon the men who had come under

the spell of the religious revival. They flocked into the
combinations and threw their heart and soul into the
movement. Many of them became leaders and performed
their tasks as if engaged in a religious revival. It was
surely a new evangel, worthy of great effort and sacrifice.
What these men meant to Trade Unionism has not yet
been fully portrayed or recognized. But it can be asserted
with confidence that while religious men of the first and
second generations remained at the helm, the ethical and
moral aspects of the movement would take an important
place. The danger now is that these aspects may be
supplanted by the political.

While men believed in the justice of their cause, in the
righteousness of their claim, they could have the assurance
of Divine support, that God was on their side, and right
would ultimately win. In fact they could pray for God's
help, as did the miners of Durham and Northumberland
in the strikes of 1831, 1832, and 1844. These miners
under the guidance of the Ranter preachers had regular
prayer-meetings, some of them by the road-side, to pray
for success in their conflicts with the coal-owners.

Tommy Hepburn (1795-1864), who initiated 'the first
great union of Northern miners in 1831 and conducted the
strike of 1832 with great forbearance and ability', spent
his life 'in advocating shorter hours of labour and ex-
tended education for miners'. He was a Primitive
Methodist local preacher and knew the value of prayer.[3]
On one occasion he went to Newcastle to meet Lord
Londonderry in order to settle the strike of 1831. At the
beginning of the negotiations he told his Lordship that
he never entered upon matters of that kind without first
asking for divine guidance. He thereupon asked his
Lordship to kneel down while he prayed. The miners
gained an important victory that day. Their hours of
labour per day were reduced for the first time to twelve.

[3] *Minutes of Northumberland Miners Association 1939.*

Evidence of the ethical and moral aspects are found in other incidents. When the Conference of miners met in Leeds at the Co-operative Hall from 9th-14th November 1864, the veteran reformer, the Rev. J. R. Stephens, an ex-Wesleyan minister, was appointed chaplain. His chief duty was to lead the assembly in prayer.[4]

When the Conference of Agricultural Labourers met in Leamington Spa in 1872 to establish a Trade Union, members were continually addressing each other in terms of Christian fellowship, such as 'My Christian Friends', 'Beloved Brethren', 'My Dear Fellow Christians'.[5]

When John Wilson and William Brown were sent as Trade Union missionaries by the Durham miners in 1878 to the Midlands to organize Trade Unions they adopted the technique of a religious evangelist; they started their public meetings with hymns and prayer and William Brown being an evangelistic singer usually sang one or two Gospel solos. 'The first meetings were held on very historic ground, Harriseahead, where the first Primitive Methodist Chapel was built.' As was natural they had the assistance of the chapel choir. 'The second meeting was held on the Mecca of Primitive Methodism, Mow Cop, and in the school there.'[6]

The struggle for existence was reinforced in the second half of the century by the adoption of the political objectives. Some of the Trade Union leaders felt that moral force was not sufficient; they wanted something more tangible. So they secured a number of unions to agitate for the franchise, and to obtain an amendment of the Master and Servant law, New Mines Regulations, National Education, and Legislation in favour of the Trade Unions. They were supported by a number of Trades Councils, the first of which was formed in 1861.

[4] S. & B. Webb, *History of Trade Unionism*, p. 302.
[5] Hasback, *History of the Agricultural Labourer*, p. 278.
[6] *Autobiography of John Wilson, J.P., M.P.*, pp. 265-6.

In 1868 the first Trades Union Congress was held in
Manchester and the Congress turned its attention to
political objectives. In addition a Parliamentary Committee was formed to watch political developments and to
exert pressure on Members of Parliament when necessary.
Some political fruits were forthcoming in the next few
years. In 1871 Trade Unions were legalized by enrol-
ment with the Registrar for Friendly Societies. In 1875
the Protection of Property Act was passed, and in the
following year the Trade Union Amendment Act.

The struggle for the rights of combination continued
throughout the whole of the century and right into the
present century. A glance at the number of strikes gives
an idea of the terrific nature of the struggle. The industrial field was scarcely ever free from conflict. From 1870
to 1879 the average number of strikes annually amounted
to 235. In the last thirteen years of the century the average
per year was over one thousand. The number of conflicts in the first thirty-seven years of the twentieth century
reached the high figure of 25,000, roughly 700 per year.
In those thirty-seven years the number of days lost
through the strikes was 334,781,694.

However long and fierce the struggle of the Trade
Unions they continued to make progress. Between 1850
and 1859 173 unions came into being; in the next ten
years, 1860-9, 118; from 1870 to 1879, 159; 1880 to
1889, 278; 1890 to 1899, 497—a total of 1,225 in fifty
years.

At the same time the organization of the unions greatly
improved. The Trades Councils and the Trades Union
Congress were exercising a growing influence. In 1889
the Miners Federation of Great Britain was established
and by the end of the century an International Congress
of Miners had been organized.

By taking stock at the beginning of the twentieth century the Trade Unions could reckon on a number of

benisons. They had acquired a legal basis. They were allowed to register their separate unions and have their funds and buildings protected. They could negotiate with their employers for the improvement of wages, hours, and conditions. They now had the right to strike to accomplish their objectives and to engage in peaceful picketing to win unity of purpose and effort.

By 1906 the Trade Unions had acquired a loyalist status and were regarded in many quarters as 'beneficial institutions'.

As respect for the movement increased so did the numbers of the various unions. In 1901 the number of Trade Unionists in the country amounted to 1,922,166; in 1907, 2,406,746; 1910, 3,987,115; 1919, 6,600,678; 1920, 6,994,078. After the second Great War the numbers rose to 10,000,000. Two wars had demonstrated their loyalty, their respect for the monarchy, and their attachment to the constitution. Now they could be trusted with political power.

When the Labour Party took over the reins of Government in 1945 the Trade Unions had come to the apex of their influence. Much of the legislation that followed bore the stamp of Trade Union influence. Benisons never before dreamt of poured into the lap of the Trade Union Movement. The Welfare State, no longer a dream and an ideal, but a splendid reality, promised a better day. Many of the important industries were brought under the control of the community and immediately wages, hours, and conditions of work began to improve. Never before have the working people been so well off—with a very little stretch of the imagination they can be designated the 'new rich'.

Labour now shares in the shaping and the making of State policies and purposes. No Government, either Labour or Tory, dare ignore the voice of the Trade Unions. They now form a vital part in the machinery of the State. They are part of the constitution and need wise men at the head of the movement. Under intelligent leadership they can make a further contribution to the political and industrial well-being of the nation and to the increasing happiness of the common people.

CHAPTER THREE

THE METHODIST IMPACT

IN MANY RESPECTS Methodism and Trade Unionism can be regarded as parallel movements and not in competition or rivalry with each other. Each in its own way ministered to the needs of the working-class population, promising suitable rewards and blessings to those that responded. For more than two centuries they pursued separate courses and from time to time contacted and affected each other.

The two movements in origin, nature, and purpose are very different. One is moral and spiritual in tone and character, the other economic and materialistic, though claiming at intervals a moral and spiritual basis and impetus. Methodism seeks the salvation of the individual soul, Trade Unionism the welfare of a particular group. The former in scope and objective is more comprehensive and abiding in its appeal, in fundamentals a classless movement; the latter is rather restrictive and confined, reserving its gains to selected sections of the community.

Both movements at the onset had to struggle hard and long for mere survival; both were resisted and misrepresented by those in authority; both needed supporters that could be strong and courageous; and both had disciples that suffered unjustly and needlessly for the causes they espoused.

Methodism being a religious movement sought the reform of the spirit in man and by so doing affected the whole of his life—political, social, industrial, religious. Its impact on the industrial side of man's life had a special significance, particularly its influence on his Trade Union activities. For more than a century

Methodism, through its members, adherents, and officials, supplied the Trade Unions, local and national, with a unique type of leadership, suitably trained and ready for service. Among all types of workers, and especially the mining community, talents were discovered and developed, fellowship encouraged, and the love of one's neighbour advocated. In the chapel they learnt to govern themselves and others; they were encouraged to use their talents, to trust in God and do the right. In these and other ways Methodism without being aware of it became a congeries of schools and colleges from which there issued men inspired and destined to lead their fellows in the struggle for economic betterment.

Recent investigation has produced a list of eighty full-time Trade Union leaders who owed their career, position, and influence to their religious experience. They became Trade Union leaders because first of all they were deeply stirred by religion.

Seventy of the 80 came from Methodism, 46 from Primitive Methodism, 14 from United Methodism (1907 Union), and 9 from Wesleyan Methodism, while one came from Independent Methodism. Fifty-five of the 70 were local preachers, 38 Primitive Methodist, 8 United Methodist, 8 Wesleyan Methodist, and one Independent Methodist. A remarkable feature of this analysis is the contribution from the Primitive Methodist Connexion. It provided more than twice as many as all the other sections of Methodism put together, although they could only count one third of the total membership.

These Trade Union leaders, outstanding in many respects, were distinguished by the nature of their activities. Those activities were never revolutionary. They were personal, political, social, religious, moral, and spiritual. The Continent had no influence upon these men. It was Methodism that fashioned and moulded their character and conduct. In some senses they were like kings among their fellows,

commanding, convincing, courageous. Some of them
appeared to have the wisdom of a Solomon; they were
wise, sagacious, and understanding. Most of them came
upon the scene like the Old Testament prophets, without
herald, and without pomp and show. They called attention
to the evils of their day, and, burning with indignation
against their masters because of the treatment of the working people, they cried: 'What doth the Lord require of thee,
but to do justly, to love mercy, and to walk humbly before
thy God.'

These modern prophets for the most part came from
lowly places and restricted circumstances. None of them
(except one maybe) could boast of a university education; none of them had been to a public school. Religion
and experience were their tutors and instructors. As
a matter of fact they never had leisure for education.
To earn a few pence a day claimed their time and talents,
as evidenced by the fact that twenty-nine of the seventy
Methodist Trade Union leaders began work under the age
of twelve.

John Batey (1852-1925), born at Backworth, was one
of them. His first occupation at the age of eleven kept
him at the pit-head of the local coal-mine. Later he
served as apprentice to an engine-wright. Interested in
Trade Unionism he became treasurer of the Northumberland Colliery Mechanics Association and in 1897 was
appointed part-time secretary. In the course of the next
ten years the work of the union greatly increased and he
was appointed general secretary, a full-time task. Other
interests occupied his attention and he became treasurer
of the National Federation of Colliery Mechanics.

Early in life he became a member of the Primitive
Methodist Connexion and immediately began to exercise
his talents. He accepted the office of a Sunday-school
teacher and also that of a local preacher, holding the
latter office fifty years.

By marriage he belonged to Primitive Methodism. His wife was the sister of the Rev. Matthew Johnson, a notable Primitive Methodist Minister, and of John Johnson, M.P. for Gateshead, 1904-10, and a local preacher.

Samuel Coulthard (1853-1931), born at Coxhoe, County Durham, was another who began work at the age of eleven. He belonged to a numerous family and following the custom of the village he went down the mine. After passing through the various grades of work he finally became a deputy. Taking a keen interest in Trade Unionism he assisted in the organizing of a union among the deputies. In recognition of his services and character he was appointed part-time secretary of the Northumberland Deputies Association, and after six years became the full-time secretary in 1907, retaining the post until 1931.

Samuel Coulthard in religion was a Free Methodist and at Seghill he threw himself heart and soul into the work, as a Sunday-school teacher and a local preacher. William Straker who knew him well wrote of him: 'First, last, and always, Sam Coulthard was a servant of Jesus Christ. . . . I knew him as a Christian indeed, who loved God and his neighbour. His last words he uttered before he went home were: "Good night, good night everybody. . . . In that shadowless day we will meet again." ' [1]

William Straker (1855-1941), born at Snittar, near Rothbury, was the son of an agricultural labourer. He, too, became a wage-earner at the age of eleven. His first job was on the land and his second down the mine. At the age of seventeen he registered as a member of the miners' lodge, and seven years later (1879) he was appointed delegate for the Widdrington Lodge. In 1882 he became a member of the county executive and in 1905 general secretary of the Northumberland Miners Association. When he relinquished his position in 1935 he had given more than fifty years service to the Trade Union Move-

[1] *Minutes of Northumberland Miners Association* (1931), pp. 9, 119-24.

ment in the county, the country, and the Continent. Although restricted in his early years because of the lack of education, he ultimately became an authority in Trade Unionism and political affairs. His knowledge covered a wide field; history, biography, fiction, theology, politics, Co-operation, sociology, economics, literature, science, art, metaphysics, and speculative philosophy. He stood out as an expert on the question of nationalization and presented the miners' case at the Sankey Commission. In his *Monthly Circular* to the miners in his own county he wrote on all manner of subjects, political, military, economic, and theological. He was a stalwart Christian among the Primitives and everybody knew it. He was like so many others, a local preacher.

Under the headline 'A New Year's Wish' he wrote in his *Monthly Circular* in 1917: 'I like to think of that early morn when the women from Galilee visited the sepulchre of Jesus and were told by the angel, "He is not here, but is risen". So I would say to all bereaved ones: "Do not think of your soldier lad as lying in an unknown grave in France or elsewhere, he is not there, he is risen."

> *'Oh, listen now ye men of strife,*
> *And hear the angels sing.'*

Seven of the Trade Union leaders started work at the age of ten. Thomas Burt (1837-1922) was one of them. Born at Murton Row, he moved with his parents to Haswell Colliery in 1847 because of a strike at Seaton Delaval. While at Haswell Colliery he started work in the coal-mine. In the next eighteen years he passed through all the grades of a miner's life and in 1865 he took off his pit-clothes and became the general secretary of the newly-formed union, the Northumberland Miners Mutual Confident Association.

As a Trade Unionist Thomas Burt's influence was paramount in the organizing of the Northumberland Miners

Association, the National Union of Miners, and the International Congress of Miners.

In working-class politics he was outstanding. He entered Parliament in 1874 and remained a member until his death in 1922. Entrusted with office as Secretary of the Board of Trade (1892-5) he showed by his demeanour and influence that the Government of the day had nothing to fear from the representatives of the working-class population. He was no revolutionary and 'tub-thumper'. In fact he was 'the gentle-voiced' reformer and politician.

All this can be explained in a simple way. He was brought up in a Primitive Methodist home. His father and an uncle were local preachers, and another uncle a class leader. He was an adherent of the Primitives and came under the influence of some notable Primitive Methodist ministers. It is no exaggeration to say that he carried the Methodist influence into every branch of his work and its effects were seen and felt in many ways, especially in his character.

William House (1854-1917) was another who started work at the age of ten. At first he was a labourer at West Auckland Colliery and three years later he descended the mine. Having worked his way through the various grades he became a coal hewer at the age of nineteen.

The urge to self-improvement came to him on joining the Primitive Methodists and he applied himself to serious study, by and by acquiring the status of a local preacher. Up to manhood he had little schooling but through the medium of his religion he got a passion for learning and desire to engage in service for the community. Every movement, educational, industrial, social and religious had his enthusiasm. In 1899 he obtained official position in the Durham Miners Association; he was made a Joint Committee Secretary and in the following year he was appointed president of the association. Seventeen years later the *Durham Chronicle* declared he had filled the office 'with honour to himself and with acceptance and admirable service to members' (11th May 1917).

Another honour came to him on 27th October 1914, when he was given the position of vice-president of the Miners Federation of Great Britain. In these tasks and in others connected with politics and local government he displayed intelligence, understanding, and statesmanship.

James Robson (1860-1934), also of West Auckland, had little chance of education. After three years at the village school and at the age of ten he became a wage-earner. Twenty years later he was entrusted with a responsible job requiring mental alertness and intelligence; he was appointed checkweighman at Broompark Colliery, then for Bearpark. In 1917, on the death of William House, he was selected as his successor as president of the Durham Miners Association.

When the fact became known the *Durham Chronicle* (7th December 1917) commented: 'Forty-seven years ago a pit lad working over twelve hours a day at tenpence per shift: Today, President of the Durham Miners Association, one of the most extensive trade union concerns in the whole of the United Kingdom. This is briefly the achievement of Mr James Robson who on Saturday was elected by representative miners of the county to occupy the presidency of the Durham Miners organization. . . . It is a responsible office and one which calls for the exercise of great ability, discretion, and tact. Such an official must have a wide knowledge of industrial subjects, be well acquainted with trades unionism in its widest aspects, and be finally conversant with all that concerns the miner and his vocation. In all these respects the miners of Durham may be regarded as having scored in selecting Mr Robson, who at 57, in his prime, is thoroughly well adapted for the tasks that lie before him.'

When the end of his service came, he was described by those who knew him as 'a striking personality' and 'a great stalwart'.

James Robson, like so many other leaders, was a deeply religious man and a member of the New Connexion Methodist Denomination.

When Peter Lee (1864-1935) was elected to the highest post in the Durham Miners Association, the *Durham County Advertiser and Durham Chronicle* commented (10th October 1930): 'The new General Secretary of the Durham Miners Association, County Councillor Peter Lee, claims to be "a native of the world". True he was born at Trimdon Colliery, but he has lived in three different countries and has visited many others. He has worked in seventeen different mines in the Durham Coalfield, two in Cumberland, two in Lancashire, and also in mines in South Africa and in America. He has the unique experience that he has resided in seventy different homes.'

How this man, who had to earn his living from the age of ten, could settle in any one place and do service for the community is a standing miracle. Nevertheless, the miracle happened, and mainly through the medium of the Primitive Methodists. They gave him a passion for learning, for service, and for religion. They taught him to speak, to pray, and to preach, eventually entrusting him with the office of a local preacher.

To prepare for all this he started at the age of twenty-one to learn the three 'Rs' and when he took his first examination, on either side of him was a boy only half his size. Yet thirty-one years later he was chairman of the Durham County Council, of the County Finance Committee, and of the Labour Party Group in the Council.

And more than that, he was the thinking, active leader of more than one hundred thousand miners, and the most mighty man in counsels touching the lives of one million people.

William Carter (1862-1933), born at Mansfield, was set to work at the age of ten to mind an engine in his father's brick-yard. As the Nottingham coalfield was developing at that time he secured work in a coal-mine. Believing earnestly in the utility of combination he formed a branch of the Nottingham Miners Association and in 1902 he became checkweighman at Newstead Colliery. Seven years later he was appointed a permanent official of the county union and later assistant secretary. In 1927 when the staff of the union was reorganized he became general secretary and held this position until his death.

William Carter was interested in other affairs. In local government he was elected a Councillor of Mansfield Town Council. He held the office of a magistrate for twenty years. In 1918 he became Labour Member of Parliament for Mansfield.

In religion he was a Primitive Methodist. For many years he ran a Bible-class and through this medium exercised a great influence on the life of the young people.

The school years for Thomas Cape (1865-1947) of Cockermouth were very brief. On reaching the age of ten he had to work in the turnip fields for a mere pittance. Two years later he went down the mine.

Following in the steps of his parents he became a Primitive Methodist and a local preacher. His workmates at the pit soon recognized his gifts and selected him as their delegate to the union at Buckhill Colliery, Broughton. Conditions in the coal-mines of those days were far from satisfactory and strikes were frequent. Being the chief spokesman on these occasions he had to suffer for his leadership and for a time he was black-listed by the coal-owners. Sometimes he walked from pit to pit, almost begging for work, and none could be had.

Circumstances, however, changed for the better and

in 1906 he was appointed assistant agent to Andrew Sharp, and in the following year financial secretary of the West Cumberland Miners Association. In 1916 he became general secretary and for thirty years he directed the movement wisely and well.

Several disasters occurred underground while he was in office and in every case he was early upon the scene and gave every help to the injured and comfort to the bereaved. More than that he appealed to the proprietors of the coal-mines and to the Government of the time to improve conditions so as to avoid further explosions.

Another evidence of the trust his comrades put upon him was in 1918 when he was elected Member of Parliament for Workington in the Labour interest. He retained the seat until 1945 when he retired.

Alfred Onions (1858-1921), born at St Georges, Shropshire, was the son of a coal-miner. Like so many other Trade Union leaders he had to face hardship and difficulty in his early days. As was natural his schooldays were few and his education meagre and deficient. At the age of ten he acquired the status of a wage-earner. At thirteen years of age he was in the mine.

In his early manhood he migrated to North Staffordshire and then to South Wales. Becoming active in Trade Union affairs he was elected checkweighman at Abercarn and in 1888 he became secretary for the Monmouth District of the South Wales Miners Federation, a position he held for ten years.

He performed other tasks with distinction. He was one of the founders of the South Wales Miners Federation and its general treasurer from the beginning. In 1898 he became agent for the Sirhowy Valley. He represented South Wales several times on the Committee of the Miners Federation of Great Britain and also on the International Congress of Miners.

In local government he was very active and was a

member for a time of the Risca Urban District Council. In 1901 he became a County Councillor for Monmouth.

In politics he served the labour interests as a Member of Parliament for Caerphilly.

Alfred Onions was a loyal Wesleyan and a local preacher for many years, and through that medium much of his life and influence can be explained.

Nine of the Methodist Trade Union leaders began work at the age of nine. Charles Fenwick (1850-1918) was one of them. He was born in Cramlington and was the son of a miner. His first job was at the pit-head, and the next down the mine. At sixteen he was a coal hewer and was supposed to have reached the stature of a man.

In his youth he joined the Primitive Methodist Connexion and soon became a local preacher. Through that office Methodism discovered his talents and gave him something to do.

When the Northumberland Miners Association was formed in 1863, Charles Fenwick had already been a miner three years, and he joined the movement from the beginning.

Being appointed a delegate his first meeting was at Bebside on 6th May 1876, and from the beginning his talents were recognized. In June 1878 he was elected a member of the Joint Committee, a committee of representatives from both sides to consider any questions that might arise from time to time. For many years he remained a member of this committee.

In 1885 he went to Parliament for the Wansbeck Division as a Liberal-Labour representative, being one of the pioneers of that movement.

As a member of the Trades Union Congress from 1888, as secretary of its committee for several years, as a delegate to the Miners Federation of Great Britain, and as a representative to the International Congress of Miners, his activities and influence were constantly expanding.

John Johnson (1850-1910) had barely reached the age of nine when he was sent into the pits. His birth-place was in a little mining hamlet at Wapping in the parish of Benton, near Newcastle upon Tyne. In 1878 he went to Marley Hill, County Durham, and found work in the pit there.

While at Marley Hill he took an active interest in the work of the Durham Miners Association. As was natural he was appointed to the executive in 1883 and seven years later he became general treasurer of the county association, becoming financial secretary in 1896.

In matters of religion he belonged to the Primitive Methodists and in due time became a local preacher. Recognizing his lack of education he set himself to work and by self-denial and discipline he mastered subject after subject until he became a proficient scholar, a man of really wide and general culture. As a local preacher he gained great distinction, visiting many parts in the North-east as a special attraction.

As a Member of Parliament for Gateshead from 1904 he clung to the Liberal faith and by so-doing met with opposition from the Labour enthusiasts. He took this opposition to heart and there can be no doubt that it shortened his life and work.

John Wilkinson Taylor (1855-1934) had a marvellous career. As the son of a blacksmith he was born at North Quay, Sunderland. At the age of nine he found employment with a newsagent, but was later apprenticed to a blacksmith. His parents died when he was quite young and he had an up-hill struggle. In 1870 he went to Ann-field Plain where he exercised a great influence. Ultimately he went to Dipton and made that his permanent home.

Interested in Trade Unionism he became the first secretary of the Annfield Plain Lodge of the Durham Colliery Mechanics Association. In 1884 he was appointed a member of the county executive and seven years later treasurer of the association. Further promotion came in 1897 when he was elected secretary, holding the position for twenty-six years. Altogether he gave forty years service as an official of the association. During that time the members experienced better wages, shorter hours of work, improved conditions.

John Wilkinson Taylor had other interests. For twenty-eight years he was president of the Annfield Plain Co-operative Society, and during that time it made increasing progress. He was an Urban District Councillor for many years, a County Councillor, a magistrate, chairman of the Aged Mineworkers Homes Association, a pioneer of the Durham County Independent Labour Party, and Member of Parliament for the Chester-le-Street Division for many years.

His character, service, and influence can be explained only by his religion. He was a loyal Primitive Methodist and a local preacher for over fifty years, and his services were in constant demand.

William Parrott (1843-1905), born at Row Green, Wellington, in Somerset, had very little education. His parents migrating to the West Riding of Yorkshire sent him at a very early age to work in a brickyard, and before he reached the age of ten he was down the mine. Before he attained manhood he had joined the Primitive Methodist Church and became a Sunday-school teacher and a local preacher. Responsibility and opportunity became an incentive to him and he gave himself to self-discipline and self-education.

Anxious to improve the conditions of the work underground he gave time and service to the organizing of a Trade Union. As was natural he was appointed to office. His first appointment was that of checkweighman at the Good Hope Pit, Normanton Common. Other promotions followed. In 1876 he was chosen assistant secretary to

Benjamin Pickard for the West Yorkshire Miners Association. Five years later when the amalgamation took place between the West Yorkshire and South Yorkshire Miners Associations he was given a similar position. When Benjamin Pickard died in 1904 Parrott was elected his successor as general secretary. He followed Pickard also as Member of Parliament for Normanton.

His influence went beyond the confines of the West Riding. It penetrated to the Miners Federation of Great Britain, the Trades Union Congress, and the Congresses of International Miners. His lack of education in his early years had been compensated by a strong religious faith.

Frederick Hall (1855-1933), better known as Fred Hall, first saw the light of day at Oldbury, a mining village on the borders of Staffordshire and Worcestershire. At the age of nine he was in the pit with no more chance of education.

Having arrived at manhood he joined the United Methodist Free Church, took office, and began the task of self-education. At twenty-four he was appointed checkweighman at Alwarke Colliery, Rotherham. In 1898 he was elected treasurer of the Yorkshire Miners Association and six years later an agent, a position he held until his death.

Interested in local government he became a member of the Rawmarsh Urban District Council, and in 1894 a County Councillor.

With the death of William Parrott he became Member of Parliament for Normanton, and held the seat long enough to be designated 'the Father of the Parliamentary Labour Party'.

William Edwin Harvey (1852-1914) met with misfortune early in life. His father died, and his mother had five children to support. There was no National Insurance in those days, so William had to go to work at the age of nine.

Another form of assistance came through a different

channel. William joined the Primitive Methodist body and very soon he had an incentive to self-improvement. He became a local preacher in the little village of Hasland near to Chesterfield.

The miners of Derbyshire were badly organized at that time and William Edwin Harvey began to associate in the organizing of the Derbyshire Miners Association. The union having prospered he was elected treasurer though he continued to labour in the mine. In 1886, however, he was appointed full-time. Interested in the wider field he helped to establish the Miners Federation of Great Britain and was appointed a representative.

In local government affairs he was a member of the Chesterfield Town Council and was chairman of the County Education Committee for a time.

In 1907 he became Liberal Member of Parliament for Chesterfield, changing to Labour in 1910. He never gave up his love for Liberalism and always believed it would have been better for the working classes if Liberalism and Labour had amalgamated.

William Edwin Harvey was loved by the people he served and when he passed away and his body was borne to the grave, 'thousands of people lined the streets of Chesterfield in tribute of love'.[2]

Enoch Edwards (1852-1912), born at Talk-o'-th'-Hill, Staffordshire, had only a slender schooling. In July 1861, when he was just over nine years of age, he commenced work in the mines. Early in 1870, interested in Trade Unionism, he joined the local lodge of the Staffordshire Miners Association, and in December of the same year became its treasurer. Five years later at the age of twenty-three he was appointed checkweighman at the Horncastle Collieries, and in 1877 he was elected secretary of the North Staffordshire Miners Association.

[2] *Minutes of Northumberland Miners Association* (1914); also William Hallam, *Miners' Leaders*, p. 42

Always a Trade Union enthusiast, he helped in the formation of the Midland Miners Federation, established in 1886, and became its president. He also assisted in the organizing of the Miners Federation of Great Britain and was treasurer from the start and later its president in succession to Benjamin Pickard.

Presiding at meetings was no easy task, but Enoch Edwards proved himself a capable chairman, wise administrator, an excellent leader, and a great statesman.

All his life he was deeply religious, and a local preacher of the Primitive Methodist Denomination. Life and opportunity came to him when he joined the 'Ranters'. His talents were not only discovered, they were developed as well. Responsibilities were also recognized and accepted.

Albert Stanley born in 1863 in the mining hamlet of Dark Lane, Salop, had scarcely any education, altogether about two years at an old Dame's Academy and at a National School. He was greatly indebted, however, to a Primitive Methodist Sunday-school where he was taught to read and write, to think and to pray. Before he reached the age of fourteen he was an accredited local preacher on the Oakengates and Wellington Circuit Plan. In those days he was known as 'the boy preacher'. Being somewhat diminutive in stature, he had to stand on a stool so that he might be seen and heard.

In the seventies he moved to Cannock Chase and identified himself with the Bloxwich Circuit.

Albert Stanley made a good start in most things. At the age of nine he began work in the coal-mine; at fifteen he was already the energetic secretary of a Juvenile Liberal Association; in 1884, when he was only twenty-one, he became agent of the Cannock Chase Miners Association; six years later he was elected secretary of the Midland Miners Association, which embraced Staffordshire, Warwickshire, Shropshire, and Worcestershire.

His influence and popularity among the miners was extraordinary. Through his advice and guidance many unhappy strikes were averted.

In local government he served as a County Councillor for many years and in politics he became Member of Parliament for Mow Cop, the Mecca of Primitive Methodism.

As a member of the Miners' Federation of Great Britain and as a delegate to the International Congress of Miners his influence went far beyond the confines of his own locality.

Joseph Arch (1826-1919), a village labourer and a Primitive Methodist local preacher, gained renown and notoriety throughout the land because he had the temerity to form a Trade Union among agricultural labourers. Such a thing had never been done before.

Born at Barfield, Warwickshire, he was sent at the age of nine into the fields to scare crows for the paltry sum of fourpence a day.

Farmers had not fared badly in the years 1850-70, but when the depression came in the early seventies they threatened a reduction in the wages of their labourers.

Joseph Arch was not unpopular among his fellow workmen and on 7th February 1872 three labourers came from Wellesbourne to ask him to hold a meeting for the rural workers of the neighbourhood. He immediately responded and hundreds gathered under the old chestnut tree and heard him passionately advocate the formation of a union. Another meeting was held on 23rd February, and steps were taken to adopt his suggestion. On Good Friday at Leamington Spa the impossible was achieved; the Warwickshire Agricultural Labourers Trade Union was established and a larger union envisaged. An entry in his Autobiography reads: 'Our Executive Committee sat the whole day through, it was, I think on 10th April in the Primitive Methodist Chapel at Wellesbourne

settling what further organization was necessary, and
making plans for larger united action.' Invitations were
sent to every county in England and Wales to elect representatives and form a National Union. And it was done
with Joseph Arch as the guiding and driving force.

Writing of him the Countess of Warwick said: 'Arch
was no firebrand, but rather "a village Hampden". . . .
We hailed him as "another Moses".

'One thing that helped the movement was the direct and
unmistakable religious sentiment which found expression
at the early meetings of the labourers. . . . Most of the
leaders of the strike were Methodist local preachers.'[3]

By the end of May over 50,000 had joined the National
Union. Their faith was high and this was put on record:
'The Committee believe in the justice and righteousness
of their cause, and have the firmest faith that the divine
blessing will rest upon it.'[4]

In the mind of Joseph Arch, religion went hand-in-
hand with Trade Unionism and politics. For several years
he travelled up and down the land seeking to establish
Trade Unions among the rural workers and to advocate
the extension of the franchise. In 1885 he became
Member of Parliament for West Norfolk, losing his seat
the next year and regaining it again in 1892.

Toward the end of the century in looking back upon
that first meeting at Wellesbourne, he said: 'I know that
it was the hand of the Lord of Hosts which led me that
day; that the Almighty, Maker of heaven and earth, raised
me up to do this particular thing.'[5]

Having in mind a statement by the Countess of Warwick, the claim of Joseph Arch did not appear to be
extravagant. This is what she said: 'I know of no movement . . . which accomplished so much in so short a time.'[6]

Some of the twenty-nine Trade Union leaders were

---

[3] *Autobiography of Joseph Arch*, pp. x-xii.   [4] Ibid. p. 111.
[5] Ibid. p. 402.   [6] *A Miscellaneous Magazine*, p. 333.

forced to be wage-earners at the age of eight. John Wilson (1856-1918), the first full-time secretary of that laudable institution, The Aged Mineworkers Homes Association, was one of them. Born at Doddrington on Christmas Day 1856, he started work at eight years although the legal minimum age for boys was ten.

The care of old people, now a national responsibility, was discussed again and again in some of the Trade Union meetings. The Throckley and Bedlington branches of the union led the way and they were strongly supported by John Wilson, who in 1906 became a part-time secretary to organize the movement. His wage was 25s. a week. In 1910 he became full-time secretary and set up an office at Gosforth where he had gone to reside.

The first houses were built in Red Row, Broomhill, without aid from the State and with little assistance from the coal-owners. Other homes have been erected and the movement is now supported by the whole of the association.

John Wilson, like so many other Trade Union leaders among the miners, was a Primitive Methodist local preacher and a Sunday-school teacher.

Thomas Henry Cann (1858-1924) was another who had to start work at the age of eight. He was the seventh son of a Cornish tin-miner and first saw the light of day at Chasewater, near Cambourne. For a time he was employed on the surface of a tin-mine at the princely wage of threepence a day. After four years in this occupation he migrated to Cleveland and secured work among the ironstone-miners and lived for a time at Brotton.

While here he joined the Primitive Methodists, took an active part in their gatherings and became a local preacher and Sunday-school teacher. He now concerned himself more and more with self-improvement and succeeded better than he ever anticipated.

Growing very ambitious he went to America but soon returned and secured work at Castle Eden as a coal-miner.

Interested in Trade Unionism he became popular with his workmates and in 1890 he was chosen as a delegate to the county executive of the Durham Miners Association. Six years later he was elected treasurer. Further promotion came to him when he was elected a member of the County Federation Board, and in 1915 he reached the highest position in the union. He was appointed general secretary in succession to John Wilson.

Samuel Galbraith (1853-1936) started a busy career when he became a wage-earner at the age of eight. In the course of his life he had many positions, among them, 'tapper-boy, coal-hewer, miners' checkweighman, miners' agent, urban district councillor, Co-operative Society president, county councillor, county alderman, county magistrate, prominent church worker, and Member of Parliament'. These were the 'headlights' in the life of a man who had 'given himself unstintingly in the service of the public without thought of reward'. Thus said the *Durham Chronicle and Durham County Advertiser*, 25th January 1935.

The outstanding feature of his busy life was an experience he had on 25th August 1874. 'I was converted', he said, 'after the fashion of St Paul on 25th August 1874 at 11.30 p.m. on Brandon Hill. We had been playing cricket and had won. On our return we rejoiced at High Brandon. Some went to Thornton's public-house and some to Bell's, and we all finished at 11 o'clock. I had a glass or two of beer, not more, and when on the top of that hill a voice said to me: "Is it for this thy life was given? Get thee home and devote thyself to other things." I locked myself in my mother's front room, Neither had I breakfast, dinner, tea, or supper. I was up at three and in the mine at four. I was back home at twelve, bathed, dined and went to Mr Hepple's school, where I sat down with 300 children re-learning the alphabet.'

He joined the Methodist New Connexion and was soon in active work. He made the Bible his first book and read it through once a year and the New Testament twice. In 1900 he became an agent in the Durham Miners Association, and in 1915 a Member of Parliament for Spennymoor until 1922.

William Browell Charlton (1855-1932) was a native of Chester-le-Street and began work when only eight years of age. His first job in the coal-mine was 'coupling at the flats' at Edmondsley Colliery. After a time he gave this job up and became a boiler fireman at Littleburn Colliery where he got his certificate in 1874 as a winding engineman.

His connexion with the Durham Colliery Enginemen's Association began in 1888 when he was elected as delegate by the Hamsteels Lodge to the council of the association. He soon became an ardent Trade Unionist and was appointed president, which position he held four years. On the death of W. H. Lambton in 1905 he was chosen secretary and held the office with distinction twenty years.

In the literary sphere he wrote a book: *A Fifty Years' History of the Durham County Enginemen's, Boilerminders, and Firemen's Association.*

For over half a century he was among the most active figures in the Trade Union world. He was president of the Durham County Mining Federation Board for a time, and in the most difficult period of its history, during 1926, he fulfilled his duties with great success.

William Browell Charlton was a Wesleyan local preacher and gave a son to the Canadian Ministry in Quebec.

Four of the Methodist Trade Union leaders became

wage-earners at the age of seven. Edward Cowey (1839-1903) was one of them. Born at Long Benton, Northumberland, he was only six weeks old when his father died. His first occupation at the age of seven in the coal-mine was that of a trapper boy, sitting behind a door in the darkness for fourteen hours, having nothing to do but to open and shut the door.

In 1858, when about nineteen years of age he united with his workmates to break the bond (a written agreement between masters and workmen). His activities in this connexion brought authority down upon him, and he was black-listed and boycotted. To escape the wrath of the coal-owners he went to sea, but he was soon back, and once more was mixed up with attempts to break the bond, most of the trouble being at Monkwearmouth Colliery. He was discharged again.

Moving to Sharlston in 1871 he got employment there and joined the union. For two years he was president, then became an official. In 1873 he was elected president of the West Yorkshire Miners Association, and again was president when his union amalgamated with the South Yorkshire Miners Association. He made a good chairman and had a strong voice and a fine physique.

For ten years he was on the Board of the Miners National Union, and was a member of the Miners Federation of Great Britain. He was also a delegate to the International Congress of Miners, and on one occasion saved the miners from what may have been a disastrous strike.

Like so many other Trade Union leaders he was a Primitive Methodist local preacher, and that gives force and explanation to much of his work and influence. When he was buried in Kirkthorpe Churchyard near Wakefield, on 20th December 1903, the Vicar described him as a 'consistent Primitive Methodist'.

Samuel Finney was born in 1857 at Coal-pit Hill,

Staffordshire, and was sent to work at the age of seven in the coke ovens. Five years later he had to go down the mine. Happily for Samuel he joined the Primitive Methodists early in life and eventually became a local preacher. By devoting himself to study and engaging in Christian activities his hidden talents were developed and he became a useful citizen.

Trade Unions were being formed almost everywhere among the miners and he joined in the adventure. At the age of twenty-four he was appointed checkweighman. In 1888 he became president of the North Staffordshire Miners Federation. Five years later he was assistant secretary to Enoch Edwards, eventually succeeding him as general secretary.

Prominent in local government and political affairs he was elected Councillor for the Borough of Stoke and later an Alderman. On the death of Albert Stanley he was chosen to represent North Staffordshire as the Labour Member of Parliament.

Barnet Kenyon (1851-1930), born at South Anston, Yorkshire, very soon found that life was hard and difficult. 'Of schooling he had none, but of cold and hunger he had abundance.' At the age of seven he was employed in a brickfield at sixpence a day. Migrating to Derbyshire he found work at Balbro Colliery and later at Southgate and Clowne.

Joining the Primitive Methodists at Clowne he qualified to be a local preacher. Of necessity he now began the process of self-education, discovering that he had more talents than he ever imagined. His workmates began to trust him and in 1880 he was appointed checkweighman, a position he held for twenty-six years. As a representative of the men underground he had to voice their claims and defend their interests. While he occupied the position of checkweighman he served as president of the Derbyshire Miners Association, and for ten years (1896-1906) he occupied the double position. Promotion, however, came and he was elected assistant secretary and agent to the association. In 1920 he became general secretary, a position he had well earned.

In local government and politics he displayed the same energy and understanding. For a time he was a member of the Clowne Rural District Council and also of the Worksop Board of Guardians.

His popularity was clearly evidenced when he became a candidate for Parliament; eighty-seven lodges and forty-two thousand members of the union pledged their support. As the Member of Parliament for Chesterfield he gave his best as he did in other fields of service.

William Cowen (1860-1923) followed the same pattern as most of the other Methodist Trade Union leaders, at the onset finding life harsh and difficult, conquering defects of education through religious experience, and finally rising to heights of service and achievements.

William Cowen, born at Colbeck, near Wigton, Cumberland, started work at the age of seven. As a farmer's boy his wages were meagre, the hours of work long and tedious. The work he thought might be better underground. So down the mine he went, but his health could not bear it, and he had to find a fresh occupation. Eventually he got work in the quarries and became interested in the activities of the Trade Union. Promotion was quick and very soon he found himself holding the position of general secretary of the Quarrymen's Association.

Moving to Whitehaven he began to be active in local affairs, finally becoming a Town Councillor and Justice of the Peace.

In religious matters he was a Primitive Methodist. Although at first he was deficient in education he tried to rectify the shortcoming by persistent study. He became a local preacher and through that office exercised a great influence. Other tasks were thrust upon him. In due time he was appointed class-leader, society steward, and trustee, and in all the tasks allotted to him he showed reliability and loyalty.

In one respect two of the Methodist Trade Union leaders were distinguished from all the rest; they became wage-earners at the age of six. Joseph Toyn (1838-1924), president of the Cleveland Miners Association was one of them. His first job was that of scaring birds for which he got the sum of threepence a day. At fourteen he got sevenpence a day, and out of this he had to pay for board and lodgings. He tried other jobs and finally got work with the ironstone-miners of Cleveland in Yorkshire. After passing through various grades of work he became foreman. He cared little for this. He preferred to be on the side of the workmen.

On the formation of the Cleveland Miners Association in 1872 he at once took an active part in its spread among the workmen. In 1875 he became president of the union and in the following year he was selected agent.

His activities were not confined to Cleveland only. He was active in the formation of the Congress of Miners on the Continent. In fact at a Conference of miners in Birmingham he moved the resolution to set up an international Congress. He also gave evidence before a Royal Commission on Mining Rents and Royalties. He appeared before a Select Committee on Employers Liability.

His last message to the council of the Cleveland Miners Association when he was eighty-five was: 'Tell the men to keep united; tell them to be kind to each other.' If any one sentence can explain his work and influence it is found in this. He was a Primitive Methodist local preacher and owed everything to Methodism. He gave a son to the Primitive Methodist Ministry.

George Edwards (1850-1933), the son of a village labourer, was another example of a boy becoming a

wage-earner at the age of six. Child labour was cheap in
those days when England was constantly increasing its
wealth. This poor lad had to work twelve hours a day, seven
days a week, for the paltry sum of one shilling, less than
twopence a day.

To make ends meet was a difficult task. With his
shilling a week George imagined that the family problems
could be solved. '*You won't have to cry now mammy*', he is
reported to have said when he carried his first .shilling
home. She did cry, no doubt, when the village policeman
succeeded in landing the distracted father in jail for
stealing turnips from his master's field in order to give his
children a little bit of supper. George, too must have
wept when he was taken from his poor mother to spend a
few days in the workhouse, to be a second Oliver Twist.

At the age of twenty-two George Edwards, although
unable to read, was appointed a local preacher with the
Primitive Methodists. Now he would learn, and he did.
Now he would emancipate his workmates, and he helped
to do that. He reformed the shattered union of agricultural labourers and eventually established the National
Union of Agricultural Workers.

In the course of his labours he became a Parish Councillor, an Urban District Councillor (chairman for a time),
a Guardian of the Poor, a County Councillor, an Alderman, a Member of Parliament, an O.B.E., a Knight of the
Realm.

For nearly sixty years he exercised the office of a local
preacher, being a preacher first and a social worker and
Trade Unionist after.

*These Trade Union leaders were distinguished by the things
they suffered and the victories they achieved for the commonalty.*
Most of them suffered hardship. That of course was inevitable for the pioneers of the movement. Their duties
sometimes took them on long journeys, involving numerous interviews with the men and their masters, causing

sleepless nights while nursing serious problems, seeking to heal sores of every kind, division, dispute, hostility, and heated discussion, trying to create and preserve the necessary unity, and all the while endeavouring to lift the standard of life for all the workmen and their families.

Some of them suffered through injury received in the early days of their employment.

William Crawford (1833-1890), secretary for twenty years of the Durham Miners Association, when a lad at Cowpen, Northumberland, was so seriously injured that the doctor wanted to amputate his leg, but his father firmly refused permission. For years he had suffered in health, but his indomitable spirit kept him alive. He died in harness, doing his duty. He seemed to be aware of the approaching crisis. While attending a council meeting of the miners he noted the writing on the wall. Turning to his colleague, W. M. Patterson, he said: 'I must go, I am dying.' In less than twenty-four hours he had passed away.

William Parrot, one of the pioneers of the Yorkshire Miners Association and office-bearer for nearly thirty years, early in life experienced an explosion in the mine, his life being saved by his quick action and great courage. Not knowing what lay in the darkness beyond the track of the explosion, he rushed through the fire and by so doing he reached safety. On another occasion he was injured by a fall of coal and for a time his life was in danger.

William Pallister Richardson (1872-1930), one-time secretary of the Durham Miners Association, might have lost his life at the age of twelve. An explosion had occurred at Usworth Colliery and forty-one lives were lost. William should have been in the mine, but his father had delayed his registration. The boy's father was one of the unfortunate dead and his body lay undiscovered for three long weeks. Five months later William was at work in the very mine where his father had died.

Thomas Henry Cann, had several qualifications for the highest position in the Durham Miners Association. On three separate occasions he suffered injury in the mines· Right to the end of his career he remained a popular figure in the county.

Many of the leaders in Trade Union activities had to suffer both persecution and prosecution. Tommy Hepburn, after the failure of the 1832 strike in Durham, was black-listed and boycotted by the coal-owners. He was refused employment and had to sell tea from door-to-door to eke out a living. In some places the miners were warned of the consequences if they bought anything from him. He was almost reduced to starvation and in the end he had to give up all union activities.

During the 1832 strike one of the black-legs was thrown into a pond and immediately three Primitive Methodist local preachers were cast into Durham jail. 'The first night and every night they were there, they held a prayer-meeting.' John Iley, the leader of a choir and an excellent singer, organized a choir in jail, and the chaplain made use of their services. When they were liberated he gave them each a present and expressed a wish that more Primitive Methodists would be sent to jail.

On another occasion seven lads from Jarrow, all of them Primitive Methodists and meeting regularly in class, were falsely charged with damage at one of the mines. Nevertheless, they had to suffer and they were transported to Botany Bay for seven years.

The story of the Tolpuddle Martyrs is now well known. Six village labourers were sent to Botany Bay for daring to form a Trade Union. Five of the convicted were Methodists, three of them Wesleyan Methodist local preachers.

Most of the leaders had victories. The list was formidable. To be elected to office in the union, whether treasurer, president, secretary, or delegate, either local or national, registered not only a personal victory but a victory for the commonalty as well.

Surveying the whole field of Trade Union activity one can perceive a multitude of victories of various kinds, in local and the national sphere, in the 'cold war' and in the 'hot war', in the realm of diplomacy and negotiation with the masters, in the formation of new combinations and the build-up of the old ones, in the improvement of organization and the technique of propaganda, in the struggle for existence and the right of legal recognition, in the increase of numbers and the moulding of new influences, in the individual triumphs and the collective achievements, in the assistance through official circles and support from the rank of file, in the face of topsyturvy economics and resistance by the principalities and powers.

On occasion some of the victories were recognized and celebrated. Thomas Burt, for instance, had much reason for celebration, especially for his long life and gracious influence. In 1895 the Burt Hall was erected in Newcastle upon Tyne by the Northumberland Miners Association and was designed to be used as the headquarters of the union and to commemorate the value of his work as a Member of Parliament, as a Trade Union leader, and as Secretary of the Board of Trade under the premiership of William Ewart Gladstone.

His manifold victories were further recognized and celebrated on 27th June 1911, when the honorary degree of Doctor of Civil Laws was conferred upon him by the University of Durham, and six months later, 19th January 1912, he was given the freedom of the City of Newcastle.

To commemorate the value of the service rendered by Charles Fenwick as Member of Parliament for thirty-two years and as a member of the Joint Committee for the miners of Northumberland, the Northumberland Miners Association arranged a public Luncheon in 1917. William Weir as president of the union presided, and he

was supported by William Straker the general secretary.
John Cairns (1859-1923) was there as financial secretary,
and William Hogg (1865-1946) as general treasurer.
Others present were John Humphrey (1861-1930),
secretary of the Colliery Enginemen's Associations; John
Batey, secretary of the Colliery Mechanics Association;
and Samuel Coulthard, secretary of the Colliery Deputies
Association. All were Methodists and some were local
preachers. The gathering and the presentation were a
recognition of Fenwick's great service to Labour, to the
Miners, and to the Northumberland Miners Association.

William Straker was not forgotten on the completion
of fifty years service for the miners. He too was given a
public presentation.

One day a poor orphan lad, at the age of twelve, with
sixpence in his pocket and all his belongings on his back,
set out from Stanhope in Weardale to tramp all the way
to the Cathedral City of Durham, hoping when he arrived
there he would find work to keep his weary body alive.
Sixty-six years later when he lay dying, the Queen of
England, Queen Victoria, sent him a letter of sympathy
and good wishes, and when he passed away the Queen
sent a letter of condolence to his bereaved friends. On the
day of his funeral thousands of miners and their families
crowded the narrow streets of the city, and so numerous
were the folk who wanted to pay their last respects to
their dead hero that a funeral service had to be held
simultaneously in the three Methodist Churches. The
person whose victories were honoured in this way and
by such sincerity was John Wilson, the general secretary
for many years of the Durham Miners Association.

A large number of the leaders were entrusted with civic
positions, such as Town Councillors, Urban District
Councillors, County Councillors, Members of Parliament,
and even Magistrates.

John Wilson was one of these. For a time he was County

Councillor, Chairman of the Council, an Alderman, a Member of Parliament, and a Doctor of Laws (conferred upon him by the University of Durham).

Arthur Henderson, shortly after he came to Darlington, was appointed Town Councillor, being Mayor for one year, and later became a Member of Parliament as a Labour Representative, and was secretary of the Labour Party for many years.

Jack Lawson became a Member of Parliament for the Chester-le-Street Division and later reached Cabinet rank, and for several years occupied the position of Lord Lieutenant of the County of Durham.

Peter Lee rose to one of the highest positions in the county, that of Chairman of the County Council, and received a permanent recognition when the new town erected near Horden and Blackhall was named after him, Peterlee.

Mark Hodgson, the one-time secretary of the Boiler Makers Union and Steel Shipbuilding Society, was entrusted with public office of various kinds and was ultimately knighted by the King.

David James Shackleton (1863-1938) for his victorious labours received the C.B.E. in 1916 and the K.C.E. later. He was also appointed a Commissioner of the Railways and of Public Health.

Victories by Andrew Naesmith were recognized by the University of Manchester when the M.A. was conferred upon him, by the Sovereign of the Realm when in 1942 he received the O.B.E. and six years later the C.B.E. Further recognition was given him in 1953 when he was knighted. In 1949 he was appointed to the Court of Directors of the Bank of England, the appointment being renewed in 1953.

Thomas Hepburn, the first full-time leader of the miners of Northumberland and Durham, had few distinctions, but after his death a monument was erected over his grave in Heworth Churchyard by the miners of the two counties and friends. It stands as a testimony to his gracious influence and self-sacrificing service.

Little or nothing had been said about the labours of other pioneers, Methodist in character and principle, but what has been said about the others can be regarded as typical of them, whether part-time or full-time officials.

Nor has anything been said about the Methodist impact through technique and organization, and this phase of its influence must not be forgotten. But space is limited and emphasis has been given to the more important phase, namely the impact through leadership.

CHAPTER FOUR

CONCLUSION

Watchman, what of the night? What about the future? Trade Unions have been established, more than a thousand of them, and in face of bitter antagonism. At the moment they have reached the apex of their influence and are very powerful. They seem to have obtained all and much more than they planned and struggled and fought for. But the millennium has not come. And more than that, a number of problems has arisen, and awaits solution by the unions.

For example: *What about the position of the individual?* Must he be ruled and governed by mass meetings and a psychological show of hands? Is there room in the union for a man with a conscience? Must he always be told how hard and long he can work? 'Is not the life more than meat?' Methodists believe in the dignity of human nature, in the freedom of the will, in the responsibility of the individual before God. Whatever happens the freedom of the individual ought to be protected. Without vision and the liberty of utterance, fetters do not fall, and the high-way to more gracious horizons is barred.

What about the rights of the minority? Is the majority always right? Is there something sacred about majorities? One man may be right and one hundred wrong. That was the considered opinion of a celebrated political philosopher one hundred years ago. If true then it may be true now. The inference is—the minority may be right sometimes. Trade Union leaders should be guardians of the rights of minorities.

What about the exercise of political power by the Trade Unions? Is it wise and proper to be partisans in the political field? Is it risky and dangerous to be married to a particular brand of socialistic idealism? Is it wise to be led by the nose to a subsidized school of philosophic theory?

What about the position of the Communists in the Trade Union fold? The working-class combinations were never intended to be the cat's paw of Continental revolutionaries. The Communist according to his own pledge is an atheist, a materialist, a revolutionary. One of the fundamental conditions of membership in the Communist Party is a denial of the Supernatural. He is pledged to a ceaseless conflict with what he calls capitalism until it is completely destroyed. He is therefore a revolutionary. Trade Unionists everywhere ought to ask for legislation to make it illegal and impossible for a Communist to hold office or membership in a Trade Union.

What about the influence of Methodism on the Trade Unions at the present time? Methodism undoubtedly has lost ground and in addition has lost favour with the unions, and for no apparent reason. Methodism in the formative days of the movement had tremendous success among them mostly because of its message, its evangelism, its democratic practices, and its warm-hearted sociability. It was the religion of the working man. It made use of the laymen. It must get back to these fundamentals again to win and retain the working classes. Sad it would be for England and Europe and the parish which in John Wesley's language is the world itself, if Methodism were to be regarded as having spent its passion, muted its zeal for applied Christianity, hushed its challenge in the town of Mansoul and withdrawn itself into its own walls and worship away from the problems of hearths and homes of the multitudes and the yearnings and strivings of human hearts in warfare with the world. Sad it would be, sad as the abandonment of an intense apostleship and the bliss of the dawn.

Methodism is still a friend of the working man, and in the eighteenth and nineteenth centuries his best friend. What has been in the past can be again in the future. Methodism desires to be his best friend now and deeply wishes to be his best friend in the years of destinies yet to be.

BIBLIOGRAPHY

Biography

Arch, Joseph, *Story of His Life* (London 1898)

Blackburn, Fred, *George Tomlinson*

Broadhurst, Henry, *The Story of His Life* (London 1901)

Burt, Thomas, *Pitman and Privy Councillor* (London 1924)

Edwards, George, *From Crow-scaring to Westminster* (London 1922)

Hodges, Frank, *My Adventures as a Labour Leader* (London 1925)

Lawson, Jack, *A Man's Life* (London 1933)
  Peter Lee (London 1936)

Wearmouth, Robert F., *Pages from a Padre's Diary* (Consett 1958)

Wilson, John, *Memories of a Labour Leader* (London 1910)

History

Allin, Thomas, *The Jubilee of the Methodist New Connexion* (London 1848)

Arnot, R. Page, *A History of the Miners Federation of Great Britain* (2 vols), (London 1948, 1952)

Eayrs, G., *A Short History of the U.M. Church* (1913)

Fynes, Richard, *The Miners of Northumberland and Durham* (Sunderland 1873)

Kendall, H. B., *The Origin and History of the Primitive Methodist Church* (2 vols), (London, n.d.)

Patterson, W. M., *Northern Primitive Methodism* (London 1909)

Pyke, R., *Story of the Bible Christian Methodists* (London, n.d.)

Smith, Henry, *Story of the United Methodist Church* (London 1932)

Townsend, W. J., etc., *A New History of Methodism* (2 vols), (London 1902)

Wearmouth, Robert F., *Methodism and the Common People of the Eighteenth Century*
Methodism and the Working-class Movements, 1800-50
Some Working-class Movements of the Nineteenth Century
Methodism and the Struggle of the Working Classes
The Social and Political Influence of Methodism in the Twentieth Century

Webb, Sidney and Beatrice, *The Story of the Durham Miners* (London 1921)
The History of Trade Unionism (London 1922)

Wesleyan Reform Book Room, *Origin and History of the Wesleyan Reform Union* (Sheffield 1896)

Wilson, John, *A History of the Durham Miners Association, 1870-1904* (Durham 1907)

Magazines

Bible Christian (1850-1907)
Independent Methodist (1823-1901)
Labourer's Friend (1850-84)
New Connexion (1850-1907)
Primitive Methodist (1819-1932)
Wesleyan Association (1838-1907)
Wesleyan Methodist (1800-1932)
Wesley Historical Society Proceedings (1897-1957)

Miscellaneous

Anon., *Methodism in 1879* (London 1899)

Askew, Edwin, *Free Methodist Manual*

Barnes, Right Hon. G. N., *Religion in the Labour Movement* (London 1919)

Baxter, M., *Memorials of the United Methodist Free Churches* (London 1865)

Booth, Charles, *Labour and Life of the People* (2 vols), (London 1891)

Cole, G. D. H., etc., *The Common People* (London 1938)

Gregory, Benjamin, *Side Lights of the Conflicts of Methodism* (London 1898)

Kendall, H. B., *Handbook of Primitive Methodist Church Principles* (London 1898)

Minutes, *New Connexion* (1800-1932)
    Primitive Methodist (1819-1932)
    Wesleyan Association (1841-57)
    Wesleyan (1744-1932)
    Northumberland Miners Association (1890-1950)

Simon, John S., *John Wesley* (5 vols)
    A Summary of Methodist Law and Discipline (1924)

Stevens, Abel, *History of Methodism* (3 vols.) (1858-78)

Wesley, John, *Journals*

Newspapers

Daily News (1872-3)
Durham County Advertiser (1930-50)
Durham Chronicle (1870-1950)
Newcastle Chronicle (1830-50)

Parliamentary Reports

The Aged Poor

Children in Coal Mines

Children in Factories

Cholera in Newcastle

Death by Starvation

Distress

Enclosures

Hours of Labour

Labour Statistics

Lodging Houses

Paupers

Religious Worship

Rates of Wages

Sewage

State of Large Towns

Statistical Abstract

Strikes and Lockouts

Trade Unions

INDEX

Aged Mineworkers Homes Association, 49

Agricultural Labourers Conference, 33

Amalgamated Engineers, 13

Arch, Joseph, 53-4

Background of the Trade Unions, 11-28

Batey, John, 39, 66

Booth, Charles, 23

Brown, William, 33

Cairns, John, 66

Cann, Thomas Henry, 55-6, 64

Cannock Chase Miners Association, 52

Cape, Thomas, 45

Carter, William, 45

Charlton, William Browell, 57

Cholera, in Gateshead, Newcastle, North Shields, Tynemouth, 20-1

Cleveland Miners Association, 61

Coal-mines, conditions in, 25-6

Coulthard, Samuel, 40, 66

Cowen, William, 60

Cowey, Edward, 58

Communists, 70

Condition of the working classes, 11-28

Crawford, William, 63

Depression, economic, 11, 12

Derbyshire Miners Association, 51, 59

Disease, 20

Distress, 22

   in Birmingham, Brosseley, Leicester, London, Sunderland, 22-3

Durham Chronicle, 43

Durham Colliery Enginemen's Association, 57

Durham Colliery Mechanics Association, 48

Durham County Advertiser and Durham Chronicle, 44, 56

Durham County Mining Federation Board, 57

Durham Miners Association, 43, 48, 56, 57, 63, 66

Edwards, Enoch, 51, 52, 59

Edwards, George, 61-2

Fenwick, Charles, 47, 65

Finney, Samuel, 58

Galbraith, Samuel, 56-7

Hall, Frederick, 50

Hardie, Keir, 14

Harvey, William Edwin, 50-1

Henderson, Arthur, 67

Hepburn, Thomas, 32, 67

Hodgson, Sir Mark, 67

Hogg, William, 66

House, William, 42-3

Housing conditions in Liverpool, London, Manchester, 18-20

Humphrey, John, 66

Iley, John, 64

Insanitation, 17

International Congress of Miners, 34, 42, 46, 47, 50, 61

Johnson, John, 40, 48

Johnson, Rev. Matthew, 40

Kenyon, Barnet, 59-60

Labour Party, 35, 44, 50

Laws against working classes, 26-7

Lawson, Jack, 67

Lee, Peter, 26-7, 44, 67

Lodging Houses, 19

Methodism and the Trade Unions, 37-8, 70

Methodism supplied leadership, 38

Methodist impact, 37-68

Methodist New Connexion, 57

Methodists, 66, 69